Guarding the Tongue

from the book Al-Adhkaar of Imaam An-Nawawee

With Hadeeth Verification by Shaikh Sal

TABLE OF CONTENTS

INTRODUCTION TO THE BOOK

All praise is for Allaah and may the peace and blessings be on His Final Messenger, his family and those who follow him in goodness until the Day of Recompense. To Proceed:

Before you is a chapter from the great book *Al-Adhkaar* of the Imaam and great scholar of the seventh century, Abu Zaakariyaa, Yahyaa Ibn Sharaf An-Nawawee, which we decided to present as a book in itself due to the many benefits found in it. The chapter is entitled **"Hifdh-ul-Lisaan"** or "Guarding the Tongue."

The original source, *Al-Adhkaar*, is one of the prize works of Imaam An-Nawawee in which he compiles and discusses the texts related to what is recommended and forbidden from speech, focusing on *adhkaar* (words of remembrance) and *ad'iyyah* (supplications). In the last part of the book, as he explains, Imaam An-Nawawee devotes a chapter to what is forbidden and disliked from speech, such as backbiting, gossiping, and slander. So he brings the evidences from the Qur'aan and Sunnah on the obligation of guarding the tongue from evil speech.

In recent times, this great work was checked and verified by Shaikh Saleem Ibn 'Eid Al-Hilaalee and printed in two volumes. In his verification, Shaikh Saleem provides a grading for each hadeeth as well as a discussion into the reason for the hadeeth's authenticity or weakness. Due to our desire to make the E-Book a source of easy reading and benefit, we have limited the verification of ahaadeeth to just the grade that Shaikh Saleem Al-Hilaalee has provided and the references of the Hadeeth sources they can be found in, while abridging his discussions of certain ahaadeeth in some places

We advise every sincere Muslim to read and benefit from the words of An-Nawawee on this very important topic, which many Muslims are neglectful or unaware about. And we advise them to reflect sincerely on the evidences so that they can beware of falling into sinful speech. We hope that this treatise also helps to uplift doubts on the part of those who consider backbiting and criticizing to be forbidden unconditionally, as Imaam An-Nawawee explains the situations in which talking about someone in his absence is permissible, as well as the proper guidelines for that.

Lastly, we ask Allaah to make this treatise serve as a source of knowledge for those unaware about the rulings on guarding the tongue and likewise, that He make this a reminder for those who know yet are neglectful.

Written by: isma'eel alarcon
for al-manhaj.com
on January 22, 2002

CHAPTER: GUARDING THE TONGUE

Allaah the Most High says:

$$\text{مَّا يَلْفِظُ مِن قَوْلٍ إِلَّا لَدَيْهِ رَقِيبٌ عَتِيدٌ}$$

"Not a word does one utter, except that there is an (angel) Watching, Ready to record it." [Surah Qaaf: 18]

And He says:

$$\text{إِنَّ رَبَّكَ لَبِالْمِرْصَادِ}$$

"Verily, your Lord is Ever-Watchful." [Surah Al-Fajr: 14]

I have mentioned previously, what Allaah made easy for me from the recommended types of remembrances. I also wanted to include along with that, the things that are disliked and forbidden in one's speech. This is in order that this book can be complete in regards to the ruling s concerning one's verbal statements, and comprehensive in regards to explaining their different categories. So I will mention some aspects about them that every Muslim must be aware of. A majority of the things I will state here are already well known, and for this reason, I will not include the evidences for most of them. Thus, with Allaah lies the success.

Know that every individual who falls under the category of being responsible for his actions (*mukallaf*) must guard his tongue from ***all types of speech***, except for that speech which consists predominantly of some benefit. So in the situation that speaking and refraining from speech are both found to contain the same amount of benefit within them, then the Sunnah is to refrain from it, altogether. This is because the allowable speech (equal in benefit and harm) paves the way towards that which is forbidden as well as disliked. Rather, in most cases, this ***will*** be the result, and applying safety, at that point, will not be able to soothe it in the least.

Abu Hurairah (*radyAllaahu 'anhu*) reported that the Prophet (*sallAllaahu 'alayhi wa sallam*) said: **"Whosoever believes in Allaah and the Last Day, then let him speak good or remain silent."** [1]

---

[1] **Saheeh** - Reported by Al-Bukhaaree (11/308 of *al-Fath*) and Muslim (47)

This hadeeth, of which the scholars have agreed upon its authenticity, is a clear-cut proof that one should not talk, unless his speech is good – and that is the speech that consists predominantly of benefit. So if one has doubt as to whether or not his speech consists of benefit, then he should not speak.

Imaam Ash-Shaafi'ee (*rahimahullaah*) said: "When one desires to talk, then it is upon him to think before he speaks. If there is beneficial good in what he will say, then he should speak. And if he has doubt about that, then he must not speak until he clears that doubt (by making his speech good)."

Abu Moosaa Al-Ash'aree (*radyAllaahu 'anhu*) reported: "I said: 'O Messenger of Allaah! Which of the Muslims is best?' He (*sallAllaahu 'alayhi wa sallam*) responded: **'He whose tongue and hand the Muslims are safe from.'''** [2]

Sahl Ibn Sa'ad (*radyAllaahu 'anhu*) reported that Allaah's Messenger (*sallAllaahu 'alayhi wa sallam*) said: **"Whoever can guarantee for me (that he will guard) what is between his jaws (tongue) and what is between his legs (private parts), I will guarantee for him Paradise."** [3]

Abu Hurairah (*radyAllaahu 'anhu*) reported that he heard the Prophet (*sallAllaahu 'alayhi wa sallam*) say: **"Indeed, the servant (of Allaah) will speak a word, while being unaware of (its consequences), and due to it, he will be cast into the Hellfire, farther than the distance between the east and the west."** [4]

In the narration of Al-Bukhaaree, there only occur the words: **"farther than the distance between the west"** without mentioning the east. The meaning of **"while being unaware"** is that he does not stop to consider whether his speech is good or not.

Abu Hurairah (*radyAllaahu 'anhu*) reported that the Prophet (*sallAllaahu 'alayhi wa sallam*) said: **"Indeed, the servant will speak words that are pleasing to Allaah, due to which he will be given a condition in which Allaah will raise him many levels. And indeed, the servant will speak words that are displeasing to Allaah, due to which he will not be given a good condition, but (instead) be thrown into the Hellfire."** [5]

It is reported in the Muwatta of Imaam Maalik and the books of At-Tirmidhee and Ibn Maajah from Bilaal Ibn Al-Haarith Al-Muznee (*radyAllaahu 'anhu*) that the Messenger of

---

[2] **Saheeh** - Reported by Al-Bukhaaree (1/54 of *al-Fath*) and Muslim (42)
[3] **Saheeh** - Reported by Al-Bukhaaree (11/308 of *al-Fath*)
[4] **Saheeh** - Reported by Al-Bukhaaree (11/308 of *al-Fath*) and Muslim (2988)
[5] **Saheeh** - Reported by Al-Bukhaaree (11/308 of *al-Fath*)

Allaah (*sallAllaahu 'alayhi wa sallam*) said: **"Indeed, a man will speak with words that are pleasing to Allaah and by which he is not aware of what he has attained by it. Due to it, Allaah will record for him His Contentment (for him) until the day that he encounters Him. And indeed, a man will speak with words that are displeasing to Allaah by which he is not aware of what he has attained by it. Due to it, Allaah will record for him His Discontentment (with him) until the day that he encounters Him."** [6]

Sufyaan Ibn 'Abdillaah (*radyAllaahu 'anhu*) reported that he said: "O Messenger of Allaah, tell me of a matter that I may hold fast onto." He (*sallAllaahu 'alayhi wa sallam*) said: **"Say: 'I believe in Allaah', and then remain steadfast (on that)."** I said: 'O Messenger of Allaah, what is the most serious thing that I should fear for myself?" So he took a hold of his tongue and said: **'This.'"** [7]

At-Tirmidhee said: "This hadeeth is hasan saheeh."

Ibn 'Umar (*radyAllaahu 'anhumaa*) reported that Allaah's Messenger (*sallAllaahu 'alayhi wa sallam*) said: **"Do not talk much without remembering Allaah, for indeed, too much talk without the remembrance of Allaah hardens the heart. And indeed the people who are farthest away from Allaah are the ones who have hardened hearts."** [8]

Abu Hurairah (*radyAllaahu 'anhu*) reported that the Messenger of Allaah (*sallAllaahu 'alayhi wa sallam*) said: **"Whosoever is granted protection by Allaah from the evil**

---

[6] **Saheeh** - Reported by At-Tirmidhee (2420 of *Tuhfah al-Ahwadhee*), Ibn Maajah (3970), and Maalik (2/985) from the path of Muhammad Ibn 'Amr.

[7] **Saheeh** - Reported by At-Tirmidhee (2522 of *at-Tuhfah*), Ibn Maajah (3972) and Ahmad (3/413) from the path of Az-Zuhree on Muhammad Ibn 'Abdir-Rahmaan Ibn Maa'iz on Sufyaan Ibn 'Abdillaah ath-Thaqafee. Muslim (2/8-9 of *Sharh Nawawee*) reported it from the path of Hishaam Ibn 'Urwah...Altogether, the hadeeth is authentic due to its **different paths of narration.** I am surprised that the author didn't attribute this hadeeth to Saheeh Muslim when it is found in it.

[8] **Da'eef** - Reported by At-Tirmidhee (2523 and 2524) from the path of Ibraaheem Ibn 'Abdillaah Ibn Haatib on 'Abdullaah Ibn Deenaar from Ibn 'Umar. At-Tirmidhee said: "This is a strange hadeeth, we do not know of it except from the narration of Ibraaheem Ibn 'Abdillaah Ibn Haatib." I say: He is Ibn 'Abdillaah Ibn al-Haarith Ibn Haatib al-Jumhee. Ibn Abee Haatim mentioned him in *Al-Jarh wat-Ta'deel* (2/110) but neither approved of nor criticized him. Adh-Dhahabee mentioned him in *Meezaan al-'Itidaal* (1/41) and mentioned this report from him as being one of his lone reports. Then he said: "I don't know of any *jarh* (criticism) against him." I say: A lack of knowing if a *jarh* on him exists does not necessitate that he declares him to be reliable. Imaam Maalik mentioned this narration in his *Muwatta* (2/986) as a saying of 'Eesaa bin Maryam.

of what is between his jaws and from the evil of what is between his legs, will enter Paradise." At-Tirmidhee said the hadeeth was hasan. [9]

'Uqbah Ibn 'Aamir (*radyAllaahu 'anhu*) reported: "I said: 'O Messenger of Allaah, how does one attain salvation?' He (*sallAllaahu 'alayhi wa sallam*) responded: **'Restrain your tongue, remain in your home and weep over your sins.'"** [10]

Abu Sa'eed Al-Khudree (*radyAllaahu 'anhu*) reported that the Prophet (*sallAllaahu 'alayhi wa sallam*) said: **"When the Son of Aadam wakes from his sleep, all of his body parts seek refuge from his tongue, saying: 'Fear Allaah with regard to us, for indeed we are part of you. So if you are upright, then we will be upright and if you are corrupt, then we shall be corrupt."** [11]

Umm Habeebah (*radyAllaahu 'anhaa*) reported that the Prophet (*sallAllaahu 'alayhi wa sallam*) said: **"Every speech of the Son of Aadam is against him not for him, except for commanding good and forbidding evil or the remembrance of Allaah, may He be Exalted."** [12]

Mu'aadh Ibn Jabal (*radyAllaahu 'anhu*) reported: "I said: 'O Messenger of Allaah! Tell me of an act that will take me to Paradise and keep me away from the Hellfire.' He said: **'You have asked me about a major matter. But it is easy for he whom Allaah, may He be Exalted, makes it easy for. You must worship Allaah, associating nothing with him. You must perform the prayers and pay the Zakaat. You must fast in Ramadaan and perform the Hajj to the House (Ka'abah).'** Then he

---

[9] **Saheeh** - Reported by At-Tirmidhee (2521 of *at-Tuhfah*) from the path of Ibn 'Ijlaan from Abu Haazim. I say: Its chain is hasan because Muhammad Ibn 'Ijlaan is honest. Muslim transmitted from him for his supporting reports. So the hadeeth is *saheeh* (authentic) due to its supporting evidences.

[10] **Saheeh** - Reported by Ibn Al-Mubaarak in *az-Zuhd* (134) and from him Ahmad (5/259) and At-Tirmidhee (2517 of *at-Tuhfah*) from the path of 'Ubaydullaah Ibn Zuhr from 'Alee Ibn Yazeed. I say: Its chain of narration is very weak, because there are two defects in it. Firstly, 'Ubaydullaah Ibn Zuhr has weakness in him, and Secondly, 'Alee Ibn Yazeed is very weak. However, Ahmad (4/148) reported it from the path of Mu'aadh Ibn Rifaa'ah on 'Alee Ibn Yazeed. So the first defect is uplifted because Mu'aadh is honest. Also, At-Tabaraanee (sec. 59) reported it from the path of Ibn Thawbaan from his father from Al-Qaasim from Abu Umaamah. Its chain is hasan, so the second defect is removed.

[11] **Hasan**- Reported by At-Tirmidhee (2518 of *at-Tuhfah*), Ahmad (3/95-96), Ibn Al-Mubaarak in *az-Zuhd* (1012) and others, from the path of Hamaad Ibn Zayd from Abu Suhbaa from Sa'eed Ibn Jubair. Its chain is hasan (acceptable), the reporters are all reliable except for Abu Suhbaa. His name is Suhaib and he was the freed slave of Ibn 'Abbaas. Abu Zur'ah and Ibn Hibbaan declared him to be reliable and many have reported from him, thus his hadeeth are acceptable.

[12] **Da'eef** - Reported by At-Tirmidhee (2525 of *at-Tuhfah*) and Ibn Maajah (3974) from the path of Muhammad Ibn Bishaar. This hadeeth is weak because it has two defects. The first is Umm Saalih, her condition is not known. The second is Muhammad Ibn Yazeed Al-Khanees.

(*sallAllaahu 'alayhi wa sallam*) said: '**Shall I not show you the gates of goodness? Fasting is a shield; charity extinguishes sin as water extinguishes fire; and (so does) the praying of a man in the depths of the night.'** Then he (*sallAllaahu 'alayhi wa sallam*) recited:

تَتَجَافَىٰ جُنُوبُهُمْ عَنِ ٱلْمَضَاجِعِ يَدْعُونَ رَبَّهُمْ خَوْفًا وَطَمَعًا وَمِمَّا رَزَقْنَٰهُمْ يُنفِقُونَ ۝ فَلَا تَعْلَمُ نَفْسٌ مَّآ أُخْفِىَ لَهُم مِّن قُرَّةِ أَعْيُنٍ جَزَآءَ بِمَا كَانُوا۟ يَعْمَلُونَ ۝

'**(Those) who forsake their beds to cry unto their Lord in fear and hope, and spend of what We have bestowed upon them. No soul knows what is kept hidden for them of joy, as a reward for what they used to do.'** [Surah As-Sajdah: 16]

Then he (*sallAllaahu 'alayhi wa sallam*) said: '**Shall I not tell you of the peak of the matter, its pillar and its uppermost part?'** I said: 'Yes, O Messenger of Allaah!' He said: '**The peak of the matter is Islaam. The pillar is prayer and its uppermost part is Jihaad. Shall I not tell you of what controls all that?'** I said: 'Yes, O Messenger of Allaah.' So he took a hold of his tongue, and said: '**Restrain this!'** I said: 'O Prophet of Allaah, will we be held accountable for what we say?' He (*sallAllaahu 'alayhi wa sallam*) said: "**May your mother be bereaved of you, O Mu'aadh! Is there anything that causes people to be dragged on their faces** – or he said – **on their noses into Hellfire other than the harvests of their tongues?**"' [13]

Abu Hurairah (*radyAllaahu 'anhu*) reported that the Prophet (*sallAllaahu 'alayhi wa sallam*) said: "**From the goodness of an individual's Islaam is that he abandons (talking about) those things which do not concern him.**" [14]

---

[13] **Saheeh** - Reported by At-Tirmidhee (2616), Ibn Maajah (2973) and Ahmad (5/231) from the path of Mu'amar from 'Aasim Ibn Abee Nujood from Abu Waa'il. Ahmad (5/235-236 and 245-246) also reported it from the path of Shahr. I say: Its chain is weak because Shahr had bad memory. Ahmad (5/234) also reported from the path of Ibn Al-Mugheerah. I say: Its chain is weak because Abu Bakr (one of the narrators in chain), who is 'Abdullaah Ibn Abee Maryam Ash-Shaamee used to mix up in his narrations. But the rest of the narrators are reliable. So these various paths of narration strengthen one another, Allaah willing.

[14] **Saheeh** - Reported by Maalik (2/903) and from his path, At-Tirmidhee (2420), which is: From Ibn Shihaab from 'Alee Ibn Al-Husayn from 'Alee. I say: The narrators of this chain are reliable except that the hadeeth is in *mursal* form. At-Tirmidhee (2419) and Ibn Maajah (2976) reported it from the path of Al-Awzaa'ee. I say: This chain is hasan, its narrators are all reliable except Qurrah Ibn 'Abdir-Rahmaan

'Abdullaah Ibn 'Amr Ibn Al-'Aas (*radyAllaahu 'anhu*) narrated that the Prophet (*sallAllaahu 'alayhi wa sallam*) said: **"Whoever remains silent is saved."** [15]

This hadeeth's chain of narrators is weak. I only mention it here, to expose its weakness, since it is a very well known hadeeth. The authentic *ahaadeeth* similar to what I have mentioned here are many and sufficient for one who is granted success. I will mention some words on this regard in the section of Backbiting, and with Allaah lies the success.

As for the narrations reported on the Salaf concerning this matter, then they are also abundant. There is no need for mentioning them after having heard the previous reports. However, we will briefly inform of some of them.

It has reached us that Qass Ibn Saa'ada and Aktham Ibn Sayfee once met and one of them said to the other: "How many defects were you able to find in the son of Aadam?" The other responded: "They are too numerous to count, however, the defects that I was able to account for numbered eight thousand. I also discovered one thing which if put into practice, all of these defects would be kept hidden." He asked: "What is it?" He responded: **"Guarding the tongue."**

Abu 'Alee Al-Fudayl Ibn 'Iyyaad (*rahimahullaah*) said: "Whoever limits his speech to be in accordance with his actions, will minimize his speech on that which doesn't concern him."

Imaam Ash-Shaafi'ee (*rahimahullaah*) said to his student Rabee': "O Rabee'! Do not speak about things that do not concern you, for indeed every time that you speak a word, it takes control of you and you do not have control of it!"

'Abdullaah Ibn Mas'ood (*radyAllaahu 'anhu*) said: "There is nothing that deserves to be imprisoned more than the tongue."

Others have stated: "The example of the tongue is like that of a savage beast. If you do not lock it up, it will set out against you."

Ibn Haywa'eel. In summary, the hadeeth is authentic due to other reports and it has supporting evidences from a group of the Companions..

[15] **Saheeh** - Reported by At-Tirmidhee (2618), Ad-Daarimee (2/99) and Ahmad (2/159 and 177) from several paths of narration from Ibn Lahee'ah. At-Tirmidhee said: "A strange hadeeth, we don't know of it except from the report of Ibn Lahee'ah." He means by this that the hadeeth is weak because of Ibn Lahee'ah's bad memory. And the author (An-Nawawee) agreed with him. However some have narrated from Ibn Lahee'ah of which their report from him is authentic. Ibn Al-Mubaarak reported it in his *az-Zuhd* (385) and so did Ibn Wahb in his *al-Jaami'* (2/85). In summary, the hadeeth is authentic.

Abul-Qaasim Al-Qushayree said in his famous *Risaalah*: "Remaining silent is salvation and that is a fundamental principle. And staying quiet at the proper time is a characteristic of manhood, just as speaking when it is proper to speak is from the most honorable of matters."

And he (*rahimahullaah*) said: "I heard Abu 'Alee Ad-Daqaaq say: 'Whoever remains silent concerning the truth, then he is a silent devil.'"

He also said: "As for the preference of those who strive in good to remain silent, then that is because of what they know of the bad consequences that result from talking and from the soul's being pleased with that. It is also because of the praiseworthy attributes that will show (by doing this) and because it will incline him towards distinguishing between its types – whether good speech or its opposite. This is the characteristic of those endowed with religious devotion. And this is one of their pillars with regard to educating the people. What has been recited of poetry in this regard is:

"Guard your tongue O mankind
And do not let it bite you, for indeed it is a snake
How many people in the graveyards are there, who were killed by their tongues
Whoever fears meeting Him (on the Day of Judgement) is truly the brave one."

THE PROHIBITION OF BACKBITING AND GOSSIPING

Know that these two matters are from the most vilest and despicable of things, yet the most widely spread amongst mankind, such that no one is free from them except for a few people. Thus, I begin with these two, due to the public's need for being warned of them.

As for Backbiting (*gheebah*), then it is when you mention something about a person (in his absence), that he hates (to have mentioned), whether it is about: His body, his religious characteristics, his worldly affairs, his self, his physical appearance, his character, his wealth, his child, his father, his wife, his servant, his slave, his turban, his attire, his manner of walking, his smile, his dissoluteness, his frowning, his cheerfulness or anything else related to the above. Likewise, it is the same whether you mention that about him with words, through writings, or whether you point or indicate him by gesturing with your eyes, hand or head.

As for the body, then it is when you say: "he is blind", "he limps", "he is bleary-eyed", "he is bald", "he is short", "he is tall", "he is black", "he is yellow". As for his religious qualities, then it is when you say: "he is a sinner", "he is a thief", "he is a betrayer", "he is an oppressor", "he takes the prayer lightly", "he is lenient with impurities", "he does not behave well towards his parents", "he does not pay the Zakaat duly", and "he does not avoid backbiting." As for the worldly matters, then it is when you say: "he has poor manners", "he's unmindful of people", "he does not think that anyone has a right over him", "he talks too much", "he eats and sleeps too much", "he sleeps at the wrong times", "he sits in places he does not belong in."

As for those matters connected with one's parents, then it is when you say: "his father is a sinner", "an Indian", "a Nabatean", "a Negro", "a loafer", "a seedsman", "a cattle dealer", "a carpenter", "a blacksmith", "a weaver." As for his character, then it is when you say: "he has bad manners", "he is arrogant", "he is quarrelsome", "he is rash and hasty", "he is tyrannical", "he is feeble", "he has a weak heart", "he is irresponsible", "he is dismal", "he is dissolute", etc. As for the garment: "it has wide sleeves", "it has short hems", "what a filthy garment", and so on.

The remaining categories can be deduced based upon what we have mentioned, considering that the source rule behind it is: "Mentioning some aspect about him that he hates to have mentioned." Imaam Abu Haamid Al-Ghazaalee quoted the consensus of the Muslim scholars with regard to backbiting being: "One's mentioning something about other people (in their absence), which they hate to have mentioned." The authentic hadeeth clarifying this will be stated later.

As for Gossiping (*nameemah*), then it is when one conveys and carries the talk of people from one group of individuals to another with the intent of causing discord between the two of them.

These are the definitions of the two. As for their rulings, then they are forbidden according to the unanimous agreement of the Muslim scholars. The clear evidences in the Qur'aan, the Sunnah and the consensus of the ummah indicate its prohibition. Allaah says:

$$\text{وَلَا يَغْتَب بَّعْضُكُم بَعْضًا}$$

"And do not backbite one another." [Surah Al-Hujuraat: 12]

And He says:

$$\text{وَيْلٌ لِّكُلِّ هُمَزَةٍ لُّمَزَةٍ}$$

"Woe to every slanderer and backbiter." [Surah Al-Humazah: 1]

And He says:

$$\text{هَمَّازٍ مَّشَّاءٍ بِنَمِيمٍ}$$

"A slanderer going about with gossip." [Surah Al-Qalam: 11]

Hudhayfah (*radyAllaahu 'anhu*) reported that the Prophet (*sallAllaahu 'alayhi wa sallam*) said: **"The one who spreads gossip (*Namaam*) will not enter Paradise."** [16]

Ibn 'Abbaas (*radyAllaahu 'anhu*) reported that Allaah's Messenger once passed by two graves and said: **"Verily, they (occupants of graves) are both being tormented and they are not being tormented for something major."**

In the report from Al-Bukhaaree, it states: **"Rather, it is indeed something major. As for the first one, then he used to go around spreading gossip (*nameemah*) and as for the other, then he used not to protect himself from his own urine."** [17]

---

[16] **Saheeh** – Reported by Al-Bukhaaree (10/472 of *al-Fath*) and Muslim (105), and the wording is from him.
[17] **Saheeh** – Reported by Al-Bukhaaree (1/317 and 322, 3/222-223 and 242) and Muslim (292)

The scholars say the meaning of **"and they are not being tormented for something major"** is **"something major"** according to their opinion or **"something major"** for them to have abandoned doing.

Abu Hurairah (*radyAllaahu 'anhu*) reported that Allaah's Messenger (*sallAllaahu 'alayhi wa sallam*) once said (to his Companions): **"Do you know what backbiting is?"** They said: "Allaah and His Messenger know best." He said: **"Your mentioning something about your brother (in his absence) that he hates (to have mentioned)."** It was said: "What if there exists in my brother, that which I say (of him)?" He (*sallAllaahu 'alayhi wa sallam*) said: **"If there is found in him what you say, then you have backbitten him. And if there is not found in him what you say, then you have slandered him."** [18]

Abu Bakrah (*radyAllaahu 'anhu*) reported that Allaah's Messenger (*sallAllaahu 'alayhi wa sallam*) said in his sermon on the day of Sacrifice, during his farewell pilgrimage: **"Verily, your blood, your wealth and your honor are sacred for you, just as this day of yours is sacred, in this land of yours, in this month of yours. Have I not conveyed?"** [19]

'Aa'ishah (*radyAllaahu 'anhaa*) narrated: "I said to the Prophet (*sallAllaahu 'alayhi wa sallam*): 'You are more than Safiyyah by such and such.' [Some of the narrators said it meant that she was short] So he (*sallAllaahu 'alayhi wa sallam*) said: **'You have stated a word, which if mixed with the water of the sea, it would surely stain it.'"** [20]

At-Tirmidhee said this hadeeth was *hasan saheeh*. I say that the word for staining (*mazaja*) means: That it (her statement) would mix with the water with such a mixing that it would change its taste and smell due to the severity of its stench and vileness. This hadeeth is one of the greatest proofs in showing the forbiddance of backbiting, if not **the** greatest. And I do not know of any other hadeeth that reaches this level with regard to condemning backbiting.

$$\text{وَمَا يَنطِقُ عَنِ ٱلْهَوَىٰ ۝ إِنْ هُوَ إِلَّا وَحْيٌ يُوحَىٰ ۝}$$

"And he (the Prophet) does not speak from his own desire. Rather, it is only revelation revealed (to him)." [Surah An-Najm: 3-4]

---

[18] **Saheeh** - Reported by Muslim (2589)

[19] **Saheeh** – Reported by Al-Bukhaaree (1/199 of *al-Fath*)

[20] **Saheeh** – Reported by Abu Dawood (4875), At-Tirmishee (2624 of *at-Tuhfah*) and Ahmad (6/189) from the path of Sufyaan Ibn 'Alee Ibn Al-Aqmar. I say: Its chain of narration is authentic; its narrators are reliable.

We ask Allaah, the Most Generous, for His kindness and forgiveness from all detestable acts.

Anas (*radyAllaahu 'anhu*) reported that Allaah's Messenger (*sallAllaahu 'alayhi wa sallam*) said: **"When I was ascended (to the heavens), I came across a people that had nails made of brass, with which they were scratching their faces and their chests. So I said: 'Who are these people, O Jibreel?' He said: 'They are the ones who eat the flesh of people** [21] **and dishonor them.'"** [22]

It is also reported from Sa'eed Ibn Zayd (*radyAllaahu 'anhu*) that the Prophet (*sallAllaahu 'alayhi wa sallam*) said: **"Verily, one of the worst forms of Ribaa (interest) is being condescending with regard to a Muslim's honor, without due right."** [23]

Abu Hurairah (*radyAllaahu 'anhu*) reported that the Messenger of Allaah (*sallAllaahu 'alayhi wa sallam*) said: **"A Muslim is the brother of another Muslim. He does not betray him, nor does he lie to him, nor does he forsake him. All of the Muslim to (another) Muslim is sacred – his honor, his wealth and his blood. Taqwaa (fear and obedience to Allaah) is right here [pointing to his chest]. It is enough evil for a person to look down upon his fellow Muslim."** [24]

At-Tirmidhee said it was a *hasan* hadeeth. I say that there is no hadeeth greater in advantage and more numerous in points of benefit than this hadeeth. And with Allaah lies the success.

---

[21] **Translator's Note:** This is a reference to backbiting, since Allaah likens it to eating a human's flesh in His saying: **"And do not backbit one another! Would any of you like to eat the flesh of his dead brother? You would surely hate it!"** [Surah Al-Hujuraat: 12]

[22] **Saheeh** – Reported by Ahmad (3/224), Ibn Abee Ad-Duniyaa in *as-Samat* (165 and 572) from Abul-Mugheerah. It has also been reported by Abu Dawood (4878-4879). In summary, the hadeeth in *mawsool* form is authentic and Allaah knows best.

[23] **Saheeh** – Reported by Abu Dawood (4876), Ahmad (1/190) and Al-Haytham Ibn Kulaib in *al-Musnad* (2/30) from the path of 'Abdullaah Ibn Abee Husayn from Nawfil Ibn Masaahiq. I say: This cvhain of narration is authentic – all of its narrators are reliable. The hadeeth has supporting evidences from other ahaadeeth reported by Al-Baraa Ibn 'Aazib, 'Abdullaah Ibn Mas'ood and 'Abdullaah Ibn 'Abbaas (*radyAllaahu 'anhum*). See *at-Targheeb* (3/503-505).

[24] **Saheeh** – Reported by At-Tirmidhee (1992) from the path of Hishaam Ibn Sa'ad from Zayd Ibn Aslam from Abu Saalih. At-Tirmidhee declared it hasan, and it is as he said. It has another path of narration reported by Muslim (2564) and Ahmad (2/277, 311 and 360) from Abu Sa'eed. The author (*rahimahullaah*) forgot to mention these paths of narration.

IMPORTANT POINTS RELATED
TO THE LIMITS OF BACKBITING

In the previous chapter, we stated that backbiting was when an individual mentions something about a person (in his absence), that the latter dislikes to have mentioned – whether by using verbal statements, through writings, or by making a gesture indicating him or pointing him out by eye, hand or head.

It's Guidelines: Everything by which one causes others to understand the deficiencies found in a Muslim, then that is the backbiting that is forbidden. An example of this is when someone tells others that "such and such" individual walks with a limp or that he walks while humped over or anything similar to that from the aspects by which one desires to narrate in order to belittle the individual. All of this is **H**araam (forbidden) – there being no difference of opinion in this regard. Another example of this, is when an author mentions a specific individual in his book, saying **"Such and such person says this..."** desiring to degrade him and dishonor him. This is Haraam. However, if his intention is to clarify that person's mistake so that it will not be followed, or to clarify his deficiency in knowledge so that he will not mislead others or have his opinions accepted, then this is not backbiting. Rather it is advice (*naseehah*), which is an obligation and which will be rewarded if that is what he (truly) intended.

Likewise, if the author or anyone else speaks generally, saying: "these people" or "this group says such and such, and this is an error" or "a mistake" or "ignorance" or "negligence" or similar to that, then this is not backbiting. **Backbiting is only when one mentions a specified individual or a specific group of people (i.e. by name).**

Also from the forbidden types of backbiting is:

When one says: "Some of the people did such and such" or "some of the scholars" or "some who claim to have knowledge" or "some of the *muftees*" or "some who attribute themselves to rectifying (the *ummah*)" or "who claim abstinence" or "some people who passed by us today" or "some people that we saw" or similar to this "...did such and such", without specifying anyone, but yet the one being spoken to realizes who the individuals are specifically, due to the speaker's causing him to understand who they are (through his words).

Also from its types is: The backbiting of the devoutly pious and knowledgeable individuals, for indeed they turn towards committing backbiting by doing it in a manner by which they cause others to understand (the person they are talking about without specifying him), just as something that is quite clear is understood. So (for example) when it is said to one of them: "How is such and such person?" He responds: "May Allaah rectify us" or "May Allaah forgive us" or "May Allaah rectify him" or "We ask Allaah for his pardon!" or "We give praise to Allaah for not having tested us with entering into darkness" or "We seek refuge in Allaah from evil" or "May Allaah save us from having little modesty" or "O Allaah, Accept our repentance", and what is similar to that, by which one will come to realize that person's defects. All of this is from the forbidden types of backbiting. Likewise, it is the same if one says: "Such and such person is being tested with that which all of us were tested with" or "his wealth is a means for that (test)" or "we all have done such an act."

These are the types of examples regarding this matter. And if this is not so, then we must refer back to the source-principle of Backbiting, which is: **One's causing his audience to understand the defects found in certain people (even without mentioning their names), as has been stated previously.** All of this is understood from the prerequisites of the hadeeth in Saheeh Muslim, which we have mentioned in the previous chapter, as well as the others, concerning the limits of backbiting. And Allaah knows best.

Know that in the same way that backbiting is forbidden for the one who speaks it, it is likewise forbidden for the one who listens to it and approves of it. Thus, it is obligatory on the one who hears an individual embarking on committing the prohibited form of backbiting, to forbid him from doing it as long as he does not fear any open harm resulting from that. But if he does fear (harm) from that, then he is obligated to reject the backbiting with his heart and to detach himself from that gathering if he is able to do so. If he has the ability to reject it with his tongue or to cut the backbiting off by changing the topic, then that becomes required of him. And if he does not do that, then he has committed an act of disobedience (i.e. sinned).

If he says with his tongue: "Be quiet!" while desiring with his heart for it to continue, then Abu Haamid Al-Ghazaalee said: "This is hypocrisy. It does not remove him from the sin he is upon. Rather, he must hate it with his heart."

If he is forced to stay in that gathering in which backbiting is taking place, and he fears from forbidding it, or he forbids it but it is not accepted from him and he cannot find a way to separate himself from them, then he is prohibited from listening and paying attention to the backbiting. Instead, his way out should be by making remembrance of Allaah (*dhikr*) with both his tongue and heart or just his heart. Or he should think about something else in order to preoccupy himself from having to listen to it. After having done this, his hearing it without listening or paying attention to it will not harm him, while he is in this mentioned state. If he is able, after this, to withdraw from them and they are still backbiting, then separating oneself is an obligation. Allaah says:

وَإِذَا رَأَيْتَ ٱلَّذِينَ يَخُوضُونَ فِىٓ ءَايَـٰتِنَا فَأَعْرِضْ عَنْهُمْ حَتَّىٰ يَخُوضُواْ

فِى حَدِيثٍ غَيْرِهِ ۚ وَإِمَّا يُنسِيَنَّكَ ٱلشَّيْطَـٰنُ فَلَا تَقْعُدْ بَعْدَ ٱلذِّكْرَىٰ مَعَ

ٱلْقَوْمِ ٱلظَّـٰلِمِينَ ﴿٦٨﴾

"And when you see those who engage in false conversations about Our verses by mocking at them, then turn away from them until they engage in a different topic of speech. But if the Devil causes you to forget, then after remembering, do not sit in the company of those people who are the wrong-doers." [Surah Al-Ana'aam: 68]

It has been reported that Ibraaheem Ibn Adham was once invited to a *waleemah* (wedding feast), so he attended it and found people there who were mentioning a man that didn't come. They were saying: "He is truly lazy." So Ibraaheem said: "I brought this upon myself, such that I attended a place in which people are backbiting one another." So he left from there and did not eat for three days. What has been recited of poetry with regard to this is:

"And restrain your ears from hearing vile speech
Just as you restrain your tongue from speaking it
Because when you listen to this vile speech
You are a partner to the one saying it, so reflect."

HOW DOES ONE PREVENT HIMSELF FROM BACKBITING?

Know that this section consists of many evidences from the Qur'aan and the Sunnah, however, I will shorten it to mentioning only a few of them. So whosoever is granted success by Allaah, he will benefit from them. And whosoever is not granted success, then he will not benefit from them, even if he were to see volumes filled with these proofs.

The main focus of this chapter is to let each individual (reading) apply all the texts we have stated concerning the prohibition of backbiting to himself and then to reflect on the statement of Allaah:

$$مَّا يَلْفِظُ مِن قَوْلٍ إِلَّا لَدَيْهِ رَقِيبٌ عَتِيدٌ$$

"Not a word does one utter, except that there is an (angel) Watching, Ready to record it." [Surah Qaaf: 18]

And His statement:

$$وَتَحْسَبُونَهُ هَيِّنًا وَهُوَ عِندَ ٱللَّهِ عَظِيمٌ$$

"And you perceived it (the statement of slander) to be something small, while in the sight of Allaah, it was an enormity." [Surah An-Noor: 15]

And the authentic hadeeth that we mentioned previously:
"Indeed, the servant may say a word from which Allaah's Displeasure is gained, while he does not realize it. And due to it, he will be thrown into the Hellfire." [25]

He must also reflect on all the other evidences we have stated in the previous chapters on guarding the tongue and backbiting, as well. It is upon each individual to attach and apply these (texts) to all of his statements, such that (he says to himself before speaking): "Allaah is with me", "Allaah is witnessing me", "Allaah is watching me".

A man once said to Al-Hasan Al-Basree: "You have backbitten me." So he said: "Who are you, so that I may know to whom my good deeds are going?"

And 'Abdullaah Ibn Al-Mubaarak said: "If I were to backbite someone, I would surely backbite my parents for they have the most right to (receive) my good deeds."

---

[25] **Saheeh** – Stated previously

WHAT TYPE OF BACKBITING IS PERMISSIBLE?

Know that although backbiting is forbidden, it becomes permissible under certain circumstances when done for a beneficial reason. The authorization for doing it must be based on a valid and legitimate reason of which in its absence, its permissibility cannot be achieved. The authorization (making backbiting allowable) can be any one of the following six reasons:

1. **<u>Oppression</u>** - It is permissible for the one who is oppressed to complain about his situation to the ruler or the judge or anyone else who holds authority or has the ability to grant him justice against his oppressor. He should say: "Such and such person wronged me" and "he did such thing to me", and "he coerced me in this manner" and so on.

2. **<u>Seeking assistance in changing an evil and in returning a sinner back to what is correct</u>** - One should say to the individual whom he expects has the capability of putting a stop to the evil: "Such and such person did this, so I prevented him from it" or something to that effect. His objective should be to look for a way to ultimately put an end to the evil. If he does not intend that as his goal, then it is forbidden (for him to mention it).

3. **<u>Seeking a *fatwa* (religious ruling)</u>** - One should do this by saying to the *muftee* (scholar capable of issuing a *fatwa*): "My father" or "my brother" or "such and such person wronged me in this way." "Does he have the right to do so?" "How shall I go about putting an end to it and obtain my right while repelling oppression from myself?" and so on. Likewise, one may say: "My wife did such and such to me" or "my husband did such and such a thing" and so on. This is permissible due to the necessity for it, however, to be more cautious, it is better for one to say: "What do you say about a man who has done such and such thing?" or "concerning a husband" or "concerning a wife who did such and such" (without saying "my"), etc.

   By doing this, the goal is achieved without having to resort to specifying anyone. However, specifying an individual by name is permissible (in this circumstance), based on the hadeeth of Hind (*radyAllaahu 'anhaa*), which we shall mention later, by the Will of Allaah, in which she told Allaah's Messenger: **"Indeed, Abu Sufyaan (her husband) is a stingy man."** And the Messenger of Allaah (*sallAllaahu 'alayhi wa sallam*) did not forbid her from saying this.

4. **<u>Warning and Advising the Muslims against Evil</u>** - There are several perspectives to this, of which one is: Declaring someone unreliable in the field of narrating hadeeth and giving testimony. This is permissible to do, according to the *Ijmaa'* (consensus of

the Muslim scholars). Rather, it becomes obligatory due to its necessity. Another case is when an individual desires to enter into a relationship with another person either through marriage, business, the consignment of property, the consigning of something to him or any other of the daily affairs. It is obligatory on you to mention to that individual what you know about the person he wants to get involved with, with the intention of advising him.

If your objective can be achieved by simply saying: "It is not good for you to engage with him in business transactions" or "in a relationship through marriage" or by saying: "You should not do this" or anything similar to that, then adding more to this, such as by mentioning his bad characteristics is not permissible. And if the objective cannot be reached, except by specifically explaining that person's condition to him, then you may mention that to him in detail. Another case is when you see someone buying a product from an individual who is known for stealing or fornicating or drinking or other than these. It is then upon you to inform the buyer of this, on the count that he is not knowledgeable of it already. And this case is not specified to this example only. Rather, it also applies when you have knowledge that the commodity that is being traded is defective. It is then obligatory upon you to clarify this matter to the buyer, if he does not know of it.

Another case is when you see a student going to an innovator or a deviant, seeking to attain knowledge from him, and you fear that may affect the student. In that situation, you must advise him about the condition of that innovator, on the condition that your intention only be for the sake of advising. And this is something in which regard many people fall into error, for perhaps the person speaking may do this (advising) because he is jealous (of the person he is warning against). Or perhaps the Devil may deceive him about this matter, causing him to believe that what he is doing is advising and showing compassion, so he believes this.

One last case is when a person has some leadership role, which he does not fulfill properly either because he is not fit for it or because he is a sinner or neglectful, etc. So in this case, one must mention this to those who have general leadership over this person, so that he can be removed and someone fit can be put in charge. Or those who have charge over him can know this about him so that they can deal with him accordingly and not be deceived by him, and so that they can make the right efforts to encourage him to be upright or to replace him.

5. **<u>When one openly exposes his acts of evil or his innovation</u>** - An example of this is when someone has openly exposed his consumption of alcohol, or his illegal confiscation of people's money and raising of their taxes unjustly and his usurping command wrongfully. It is thus permissible for one to talk about what that individual

has made public. But it is forbidden to mention any of his other defects, unless they fall under one of the categories, which we have mentioned that backbiting is permissible.

6. **Defining someone** - If someone is known to the people by his nickname, such as "the bleary eyed one", "the one who limps", "the deaf guy", "the blind guy", "cross-eyed", "flat-nosed", and other than that, then it is permissible to particularize him as such, with the aim of identifying him. However, it is forbidden to apply that to him, when one's intention is to degrade him. If he can be identified with another (more appropriate) type of name, then that is more preferable. These are the six cases, in which the scholars have stated that backbiting is permissible, if it is done in accordance to the guidelines we mentioned above.

From those who have reported similar to what we have stated is Abu Haamid Al-Ghazaalee in his book "*Al-Ihyaa*", as well as other scholars. The evidences for the permissibility of backbiting can be found in authentic and well-known *ahaadeeth*. Furthermore, there is an agreement of the scholars concerning the allowance of backbiting in these six cases.

It is reported in the *Saheehs* of Al-Bukhaaree and Muslim that 'Aa'ishah (*radyAllaahu 'anhaa*) said: "A man sought permission of the Prophet (*sallAllaahu 'alayhi wa sallam*) to enter (his house), so he said: **'Permit him to enter, and what an evil brother to (his) relatives he is.'"** [26]

Al-Bukhaaree uses this hadeeth as evidence for the permissibility of backbiting the people of mischief and doubts.

Ibn Mas'ood (*radyAllaahu 'anhu*) narrated: "The Messenger of Allaah (*sallAllaahu 'alayhi wa sallam*) divided a portion (of war booty amongst the people), so a man from the Ansaar said: 'I swear by Allaah, Muhammad did not intend the face of Allaah by this (i.e. he was not fair).' So I went to Allaah's Messenger and informed him of this. His face changed (i.e. he became mad) and said: **'May Allaah have mercy on Moosaa. He was indeed abused with greater than this, but he was patient.'"** [27]

In some of the reports of the hadeeth, Ibn Mas'ood said: "I said: I will not raise another hadeeth to him again, after this."

---

[26] **Saheeh** – Reported by Al-Bukhaaree (10/471 of *al-Fath*) and Muslim (2591)
[27] **Saheeh** – Reported by Al-Bukhaaree and Muslim and its checking has preceded.

Al-Bukhaaree uses this hadeeth as proof that a person is allowed to inform his brother of what is being said about him.

'Aa'ishah (*radyAllaahu 'anhaa*) reported that Allaah's Messenger (*sallAllaahu 'alayhi wa sallam*) once said: **"I do not think that this person and that person know anything at all about our Religion."** [28]

Al-Laith Ibn Sa'ad, one of the narrators of the hadeeth's chain said: "They were two individuals from among the hypocrites (at his time)."

Zayd Ibn Arqam (*radyAllaahu 'anhu*) reported: "We set out on a journey with the Prophet and the people suffered great difficulty (due to a lack of provisions). So 'Abdullaah Ibn Ubay[29] said to his companions: 'Don't spend on those who are with Allaah's Messenger so that they may disperse and go away from him.' He said: 'If we return to Madeenah, surely, the more honorable will expel the lowly ones from it. So I went to the Prophet (*sallAllaahu 'alayhi wa sallam*) and informed him of that. He sent for 'Abdullaah Ibn Ubay and asked him, but 'Abdullaah Ibn Ubay swore that he did not say so. So the people said: 'Zayd told a lie to Allaah's Messenger.' And what they said distressed me very much. Later Allaah revealed the confirmation of my statement in His saying; **'When the hypocrites come to you...'** [Surah Al-Munafiqeen]" [30]

Also there is the hadeeth of Hind (*radyAllaahu 'anhaa*), the wife of Abu Sufyaan, in which she said to the Prophet: **"Indeed, Abu Sufyaan is a stingy man."** [31]

And also the hadeeth of Faatimah Bint Qays (*radyAllaahu 'anhaa*), when the Prophet (*sallAllaahu 'alayhi wa sallam*) said to her (with regard to her accepting marriage proposals from two suitors): **"As for Mu'awiyah, then he is utterly poor. And as for Abu Jahm, then he does not cease to remove the stick from his shoulder (i.e. he beats his wives)."** [32]

---

[28] **Saheeh** – Reported by Al-Bukhaaree (10/485 of *al-Fath*)

[29] **Translator's Note:** He was the leader of the hypocrites in Madeenah. Upon his death, Allaah revealed verses commanding the Prophet (*sallAllaahu 'alayhi wa sallam*) not to pray the funeral prayer over him

[30] **Saheeh** – Reported by Al-Bukhaaree (8/664 and 646-648 of *al-Fath*) and Muslim (2772).

[31] **Saheeh** – Reported by Al-Bukhaaree (9/504 of *al-Fath*) and Muslim (1714).

[32] **Saheeh** – Reported by Muslim (1480)

WHAT SHOULD ONE DO WHEN HE HEARS HIS SHAIKH, FRIEND OR SOMEONE ELSE BEING BACKBITTEN?

Know that it is upon the one who hears a Muslim being backbitten to oppose it and prevent the one doing the backbiting. If he is not able to prevent him with his speech, then he should stop him with his hand. If he is neither able to do so with his hand or with his tongue, then he should get up and leave that gathering. And if he hears his teacher (shaikh) being backbitten – or anyone else who has a right over him, or if the person (being backbitten) is from the people of righteousness and nobility, then his concern with what we have mentioned above should be greater.

Abu ad-Dardaa (*radyAllaahu 'anhu*) narrated the Prophet (*sallAllaahu 'alyhi wa sallam*) said: **"Whoever turns away from (harming) the honor of his brother, Allaah will turn his face away from the Hellfire on the Day of Judgement."** [33]

And it is reported in *Saheeh Al-Bukhaaree* and *Muslim* from 'Itbaan – or as some say 'Utbaan – in his long and famous hadeeth, in which he narrated: "The Prophet (*sallAllaahu 'alayhi wa sallam*) stood up to pray, so the people said: 'Where is Maalik Ibn ad-Dukh-shum?' A man said: 'That hypocrite! Allaah and His Messenger do not love him.' So the Prophet (*sallAllaahu 'alayhi wa sallam*) said: **'Do not say that! Do you not see that he says: *Laa Ilaaha Illaa Allaah* (There is no deity worthy of worship except Allaah), desiring by that, the face of Allaah?'"** [34]

---

[33] **Hasan or Saheeh** – Reported by At-Tirmidhee (1996), Ahmad (6/450), Ad-Dawlaabee in *al-Kunnaa* (1/124) and Ibn Abee ad-Duniyaa in *as-Samat* (250) from the path of Abu Bakr an-Nahshalee from Marzooq Ibn Abee Bakr At-Taymee from Umm ad-Dardaa. At-Tirmidhee said it was a hasan hadeeth. I say: It is as he said, meaning that he intended by this that the hadeeth has a weak chain, but it is reported in other paths, which have no defects, as he explains in the last part of his Sunan. So refer to it because it is important. This is because all of the narrators in the hadeeth are reliable except Marzooq. Adh-Dhahabee said: "No one reported from him except Abu Bakr An-Nahshalee." However Al-Haafidh (Ibn Hajr) said in *at-Tah-theeb* (10/87): "I think he is the one who came after." The he said: "Distinguishing: Marzooq, Abu Bukayr At-Tameemee Al-Koofee. He reported from Sa'eed Ibn Jubair, 'Ikrimah and Mujaahid. And Laith Ibn Abee Sulaim, Israa'eel, 'Umar Ibn Muhammad Ibn Zayd Al-'Umaree, Ath-Thawree and Ash-Shareek reported from him. Ibn Hibbaan mentioned him in his book *ath-Thiqaat* (The Reliable). His place of origin is Koofah, but he resided in Rayy." And he (Ibn Hajr) said in his biography for him that he was reliable. Some students of knowledge misunderstand this from Al-Haafidh but there is no reason for this confusion, because Al-Haafidh (Ibn Hajr) thought that the first (Abu Bakr) was the second (Abu Bukair). So if these two names refer to one and the same person, as thought by Al-Haafidh, and this is what is clear to me, then the hadeeth is authentic. And if they are two separate people, then the hadeeth is hasan because Marzooq is acceptable when reported from by way of Shahr Ibn Haushab.

[34] **Saheeh** – Reported by Al-Bukhaaree (1/518, 2/157 and 172 and 323, 3/60-61, 11/241, 12/303 of *al-Fath*) and Muslim (33)

And it is reported in *Saheeh Muslim* on Al-Hasan Al-Basree that 'Aa'idh Ibn 'Amr (*radyAllaahu 'anhu*), one of the Companions of Allaah's Messenger, entered in the presence of 'Ubaydullaah Ibn Ziyaad and said: "O my son, indeed I heard the Messenger of Allaah (*sallAllaahu 'alayhi wa sallam*) say:

'Truly, the most evil of caretakers (leaders) are the oppressive rulers, so beware of being one of them.'"

So he said to him: "Sit down, for you are only from the worthless scraps of the Companions of Muhammad!" So he responded: "Was there any worthless scraps among them? Rather the worthless scraps only appeared after them in others." [35]

Ka'ab Ibn Maalik (*radyAllaahu 'anhu*) reported in his long hadeeth concerning his repentance that the Prophet (*sallAllaahu 'alayhi wa sallam*) said while sitting with some people in Tabook: "What did Ka'ab Ibn Maalik do?" A man from Banu Salima said: "O Allaah's Messenger! The (beauty) of his cloak and a self-appreciation of his finery have allured and detained him (i.e. from going to fight in the expedition)!"

Upon this, Mu'aadh Ibn Jabal (*radyAllaahu 'anhu*) said to him: "What an evil thing you have said! I swear by Allaah, O Messenger of Allaah, we do not know anything about him except good." So Allaah's Messenger (*sallAllaahu 'alayhi wa sallam*) remained silent. [36]

Jaabir Ibn 'Abdillaah and Abu Talha (*radyAllaahu 'anhum*) said: "Allaah's Messenger (*sallAllaahu 'alayhi wa sallam*) said: **'No (Muslim) person abandons another Muslim in a place where his sanctity will be violated and his honor will be lowered, except that Allaah will abandon him in a place that he would love to have His support. And no (Muslim) person aids another Muslim in a place where his sanctity will be violated and his honor will be lowered, except that Allaah will aid him in a place that he would love to have His support.'"** [37]

Mu'aadh Ibn Anas (*radyAllaahu 'anhu*) reported that the Prophet (*sallAllaahu 'alayhi wa sallam*) said: **"Whoever protects a believer from a hypocrite, Allaah will send forth an angel that will protect his flesh on the Day of Judgement from (being burned by) the fire of Hell. And whoever accuses a Muslim of anything,**

---

[35] **Saheeh** – Reported by Muslim (1830)

[36] **Saheeh** – Reported by Al-Bukhaaree (8/113-116) and Muslim (2769)

[37] **Da'eef** – Reported by Abu Dawood (4884), Ahmad (4/30), Al-Bayhaqee (8/167-168), Abu Nu'aim in *al-Hilyah* (8/189) and Ibn Abee ad-Duniyaa in *as-Samat* (241) from the path of Al-Laith Ibn Sa'ad. I say: This chain of narration is weak because Yahyaa Ibn Saleem and his shaikh, Ismaa'eel Ibn Basheer are both unknown.

desiring to disgrace him, Allaah will withhold him over the bridge of the Hellfire until he takes back what he said." [38]

---

[38] **Hasan** – Reported by Abu Dawood (4883), Ahmad (3/441), Al-Baghawee in *Sharh As-Sunnah* (13/105) and Ibn Abee ad-Duniyaa in *as-Samat* (248) from the path of Ibn Al-Mubaarak. I say: Its chain of narration is weak because Isma'eel Ibn Yahyaa al-Mi'aafaree is in it and he is unknown. However this hadeeth has supporting evidences that raise it to the level of being *hasan* (acceptable). Refer to them in *at-Targheeb* (515-520). **Important Note:** Our Shaikh (Al-Albaanee) mentioned this hadeeth in *Da'eef al-Jaami'-us-Sagheer* (5/193) as being weak, but then declared it *hasan* (later) in *Saheeh Sunan Abee Dawood* (4086). The last grading is what is correct so know this.

THE BACKBITING OF THE HEART

Know that having bad thoughts about someone is forbidden just like having bad speech about him. So just as it is forbidden for you to speak to others about the defects of a person, it is likewise forbidden for you to speak to yourself about that and to hold bad thoughts for him. Allaah says:

يَٰٓأَيُّهَا ٱلَّذِينَ ءَامَنُوا۟ ٱجْتَنِبُوا۟ كَثِيرًا مِّنَ ٱلظَّنِّ إِنَّ بَعْضَ ٱلظَّنِّ إِثْمٌ

"O you who believe, avoid much (types) of suspicion. Verily some (forms) of suspicion is a sin." [Surah Al-Hujuraat: 12]

And Abu Hurairah (*radyAllaahu 'anhu*) reported that Allaah's Messenger (*sallAllaahu 'alayhi wa sallam*) said: **"Beware of suspicion, for indeed suspicion is the most untruthful form of speech."** [39]

The *ahaadeeth* with this same understanding I have mentioned here are many. What the backbiting of the heart means, is: When the heart has firm conviction and holds bad thoughts about someone. But as for the notions that occasionally display in one's mind or when one talks to himself, then as long as these thoughts do not remain established and continuous in him, it is excused according to the consensus of the scholars. This is because he has no choice in the matter so as to stop it from occurring nor can he find any way to liberate himself from it when it does occur. This is the understanding of what has been authentically established (in the texts).

The Messenger of Allaah (*sallAllaahu 'alayhi wa sallam*) said: **"Indeed, Allaah has permitted for my *ummah*, that which their souls whisper to them, so long as they do not speak it out (audibly) or act upon it."** [40]

The scholars say: "This refers to the notions that form in one's mind, but do not become settled or established there."

And they said: "This is regardless if the notion consists of backbiting, disbelief or so on (i.e. it is pardoned, so long as it does not settle). So (for example) whoever's mind becomes flooded with thoughts of disbelief, but they are only thoughts, without him intending to have them carried out, and he then rids himself of these thoughts right after they occur, he is not a disbeliever nor is there any sin on him.

---

[39] **Saheeh** – Reported by Al-Bukhaaree (10/484 of *al-Fath*) and Muslim (2563)
[40] **Saheeh** – Reported by Al-Bukhaaree (5/160 of *al-Fath*) and Muslim (127 and 202)

We have already stated previously, in the chapter on the (internal) whisperings, the authentic hadeeth, in which the Companions said: "O Messenger of Allaah! Some of us find things in our thoughts that are too tremendous to speak of." So he (*sallAllaahu 'alayhi wa sallam*) said: **"That is the confirmation of Faith."** [41]

And this goes for the other reports we have mentioned in that chapter that bear the same understanding.

The reason for these thoughts being excused is due to what we have stated previously that these thoughts are impossible to prevent. Rather, one is only able to prevent those thoughts from becoming settled and established in one's mind. This is why the heart's being resolute and determined on these thoughts is forbidden.

So whenever these thoughts, which consist of backbiting or any other sin, present themselves in your mind, it is an obligation on you to repel them, turn away from them and mention some excuses or explanations that will change what seems apparent.

Abu Haamid Al-Ghazaalee said in *Al-Ihyaa*: "If bad thoughts should occur in your heart, then these are from the whisperings of the Devil, which he has placed in you. So you must deny and reject them because he is indeed the most wicked of evildoers (*faasiq*). And Allaah has stated:

$$\text{يَـٰٓأَيُّهَا ٱلَّذِينَ ءَامَنُوٓاْ إِن جَآءَكُمْ فَاسِقٌۢ بِنَبَإٍ فَتَبَيَّنُوٓاْ أَن تُصِيبُواْ قَوْمًۢا}$$

$$\text{بِجَهَـٰلَةٍ فَتُصْبِحُواْ عَلَىٰ مَا فَعَلْتُمْ نَـٰدِمِينَ ۝}$$

'If a wicked person (i.e. *faasiq*) comes to you with news, then verify it, lest you harm people without realizing it (i.e. out of ignorance) and afterwards you become regretful for what you've done.' [Surah Al-Hujuraat: 6] So it is not permissible for you to believe Iblees (the Devil).

And if there is some sign that indicates that he is corrupt, yet he implies the opposite of that, then it is not permissible to hold bad thoughts (for him).

---

[41] **Saheeh** – Reported by Muslim (132); **Translator's Note:** This hadeeth shows the Companions' zeal and enthusiasm in commanding themselves with good and forbidding themselves from evil, such that they would even fight against the evil notions that passed through their minds. But as it is impossible to prevent such thoughts from occurring every now and then, they asked the Prophet about this. His response to them meant that their trying to repel these thoughts showed their strong Eemaan (Faith) and love for good.

Among the signs that indicate one holding bad thoughts (for someone) is that your heart changes with him from the way it used to be, and that you run away from him and find him to be unbearable. And that you are lazy when it comes to having concern for him, showing kindness to him and being worried when he does evil. And indeed the Devil comes close to one's heart when the slightest trace of defects show in people, and he places this in you, while you think (these thoughts) occur due to your astuteness, intelligence and quick alertness. But the believer sees with the light of Allaah. So this person is in reality speaking with the deceptions and the evil plots of the Devil.

And if a trustworthy person informs you of this, then do not believe him nor reject him, in order that you will not have bad thoughts about either of them.

Whenever some evil thoughts about another Muslim come into your mind, then let that make you increase in your showing concern and being kind to him because this will enrage the Devil and repel him from you. So he will not place such thoughts in you afterward out of fear that it will only cause you to increase in your supplication for that person.

And whenever you come to know of a defect or a mistake in another Muslim based on some proofs, which cannot be denied, then advise him in privacy and do not let the Devil deceive you such that he invites you and leads you towards backbiting him. And when you admonish him, then do not admonish him while you are happy and pleased that you have knowledge of his deficiency. So it is as if he is looking at you with the eyes of awe and respect while you are looking down at him with condescending eyes. Rather, make your intention in that to free him from this sin, while you are distressed over him, just as you are distressed when some deficiency enters in you. And his getting rid of that deficiency without you having to admonish him (i.e. on his own) should be more beloved to you than him having to rid himself of it due to your admonishing."

These are the words of Al-Ghazaalee. I say: We stated previously that if someone is presented with a notion of bad thoughts for another person, he should cut off those bad thoughts. But this is unless there is some (religiously) legislated benefit that leads to thinking (about that person) in this manner. So if such a reason exists, holding these thoughts about his deficiencies is permissible, as well as warning against them, as can be seen in the *jarh* (criticism) of certain witnesses, reporters and others we have mentioned in the Chapter on "What Type of Backbiting is Permissible."

EXPIATING ONESELF AND REPENTING FROM BACKBITING

Know that it is required upon everyone that commits a sin to rush towards repenting from it. Repentance with regard to the rights of Allaah must meet three conditions:

1. One must stop committing that sin immediately,
2. He must feel remorse and sorrow for having done it, and
3. He must resolve to not return to committing that sin again.

Repentance with regard to the rights of humans must meet these same three conditions (listed above), as well as a fourth one, and that is:

4. Taking back any oppression that was inflicted on someone or asking for his forgiveness or absolvment from that.

So it is obligatory on a person who has committed backbiting to seek repentance according to these four conditions, because backbiting involves the rights of people, so he must seek the forgiveness of the person he has backbitten.

Is it sufficient for one to just say: "I have backbit you, so please absolve me from (this) sin" or must he inform him also of what he said about him?

There are two views on this according to the Shaafi'ee scholars:

The First: His clarifying what he said (when backbiting) is a condition. So if he is absolved without informing him of what he said, the pardon is not valid, just as if he were to absolve him from (stealing) unidentifiable money.

The Second: His informing him (of what he said) is not a condition, because this is something that one will not be able to tolerate and thus forgive. So his knowing (exactly what was said) is not a condition, contrary to the example of the (stolen) money.

The first opinion is the strongest, since people have the ability to grant forgiveness for certain types of backbiting but not other types.

And if the one who has been backbitten is either dead or absent, then one is excused from seeking to be absolved from it. However, the scholars say: He should supplicate much for that person and ask forgiveness for him, as well as do many good deeds.

Know that it is preferable for the one who has been backbitten to absolve the backbiter from his sin, but it is not an obligation on him to do so. This is because it is giving away and forfeiting one's right, so the choice is his. However, it is strongly recommended (*muta'akkidah*) for him to absolve him so that his Muslim brother can be free from the harm of this sin and so that he can be successful in receiving Allaah's great reward of Forgiveness and Love. Allaah, the Most High, says:

$$ ٱلَّذِينَ يُنفِقُونَ فِى ٱلسَّرَّآءِ وَٱلضَّرَّآءِ وَٱلْكَـٰظِمِينَ ٱلْغَيْظَ وَٱلْعَافِينَ عَنِ ٱلنَّاسِ ۗ وَٱللَّهُ يُحِبُّ ٱلْمُحْسِنِينَ ﴿١٣٤﴾ $$

"Those who repress their anger and pardon people. Verily, Allaah loves the good doers." [Surah Aali 'Imraan: 134]

The proper way he should take in making himself allow the pardoning is by reminding himself that: "This matter has already happened and there is no way to remove it now. So it is not right for me to make him miss his chance of getting reward and absolving my Muslim brother."

Allaah says:

$$ وَلَمَن صَبَرَ وَغَفَرَ إِنَّ ذَٰلِكَ لَمِنْ عَزْمِ ٱلْأُمُورِ $$

"And verily, whosoever shows patience and forgives (others), that is truly from the things recommended by Allaah." [Surah Ash-Shooraa: 43]

And He says:

$$ خُذِ ٱلْعَفْوَ $$

"Show forgiveness!" [Surah Al-A'araaf: 199]

The ayaat similar to what we mentioned above are many.

And in the authentic hadeeth, the Messenger of Allaah (*sallAllaahu 'alayhi wa sallam*) said: **"And Allaah remains in the assistance of (His) servant so long as the servant remains in the assistance of his (fellow) brother."** [42]

---

[42] **Saheeh** – Reported by Muslim (2699)

Ash-Shaafi'ee (*rahimahullaah*) said: "Whosoever is sought to be pleased, yet is not pleased is a devil."

The people of the past would recite:

> *"It was said to me: Such and such person has spoken badly of you*
> *And when a youth sets out to humiliate, it is a shame*
> *So I said: He has come to us and issued an excuse*
> *The blood-money (i.e. recompense) for a sin – to us – is the apology."*

So what we have mentioned here concerning the encouragement for one to absolve and forgive a person from backbiting is what is correct. As for what has been reported on Sa'eed Ibn Al-Musayyib that he said: **"I will not forgive the one who has oppressed me"** and on Ibn Sireen that he said: **"I will not forbid it on him and then make it allowable for him, because Allaah has made backbiting forbidden on him and I am not going to make permissible what Allaah has forbidden, ever"** then it is either unauthentic or erroneous.

This is because a person that pardons someone is not making something forbidden permissible. Rather, he is only forfeiting a right that is established for him. The texts of the Qur'aan and the Sunnah indicate clearly that it is recommended to forgive and forfeit one's rights, which are specific to this case. Or perhaps Ibn Sireen's words can be taken to mean: **"I do not permit myself to be backbit, ever."** This would be correct, for indeed if a person says: "I seek my honor back from the one who backbit me", he is not allowing for it to be done. Rather, he is forbidding everyone from backbiting him, just as he forbids others from being backbitten.

As for the hadeeth: **"Are you not able to be like Abu Damdam – when he would go out from his home, he would say: 'I am giving my honor away in charity for the people.'"** Meaning: I will not seek justice from those who oppress me whether in this world or the Hereafter. This is useful in removing a transgression that existed before the absolvement, but as for what occurs after it, there must be a new absolvement made after that. And with Allaah lies the success.

CONCERNING GOSSIPING

We have already mentioned its prohibition as well as the evidences for that and what has been reported concerning the punishment for it. We also mentioned its definition, however all of this was brief. We will now add more to its explanation.

Imaam Abu Haamid Al-Ghazaalee (*rahimahullaah*) said: "For the most part, gossip (*nameemah*) is attributed to the one who takes the statement of a person (concerning another individual), and relates it back to that individual that is being spoken about. An example of this is when someone says: **'That person said such and such about you.'** However, gossiping is not limited to just this example, but rather its extent is: Exposing that which one hates to have exposed, whether the one he is relating from or the one he is relating the story to or the third party hates it. And it is the same if this exposing is done by speech or by writing or by gesturing, etc, and regardless whether what is being narrated relates to someone's sayings or actions, and whether it is a defect or other than that. So the reality of Gossiping is: Spreading what is supposed to be private, and destroying the concealment of what he hates to have exposed.

A person must keep quiet with regard to anything he sees (or hears) from the conditions of people, except for that which if he relates will have a benefit for a Muslim or it will prevent a sin from occurring."

And he said: "Anyone that has gossip (*nameemah*) conveyed to him, and it is said to him: **'Such and such person said this about you'**, then there are six things required from him:

1. He must not believe him because the one conveying the news is a gossiper (*namaam*), and the gossiper is a wicked person (*faasiq*), so his reports are rejected. [43]

2. He must forbid him from doing that, advise him and declare the detestability of his action.

3. He must hate him for the sake of Allaah, for indeed, he is hated in the sight of Allaah and hating for the sake of Allaah is an obligation.

---

[43] **Translator's Note** This is based on Allaah's saying: **'If a wicked person (i.e. *faasiq*) comes to you with news, then verify it, lest you harm people without realizing it (i.e. out of ignorance) and afterwards you become regretful for what you've done."** [Surah Al-Hujuraat: 6]

4. He must not think evil thoughts about the person he is relating from, based on Allaah's saying: **'Avoid much (types of) suspicion.'** [Surah Al-Hujuraat: 12]

5. What has been related to you (about someone) should not cause you to spy or investigate further into the matter, because Allaah says: **'And do not spy on one another.'** [Surah Al-Hujuraat: 12]

6. He should not be pleased for himself with what he has forbidden for the gossiper. Thus he should not report the gossip that was conveyed to him by saying: **'Such and such person told me this'**, for then he would become a gossiper himself and he would be committing that which he forbade."

It has been reported that a man went to 'Umar Ibn 'Abd-il-'Azeez (*rahimahullaah*) and said something to him about another person. So 'Umar (*rahimahullaah*) said to him: "If you wish, we shall investigate your case. If you are lying, then you are from those who fall under the *ayah*:

$$\text{إِن جَآءَكُمْ فَاسِقٌ بِنَبَإٍ فَتَبَيَّنُوٓاْ}$$

'If a wicked person comes to you with news, then verify it' [Surah Al-Hujuraat: 6] and if you are telling the truth, then you fall under the *ayah*:

$$\text{هَمَّازٍ مَّشَّآءٍ بِنَمِيمٍ}$$

'Backbiter, going about spreading slander.' [Surah Al-Qalam: 11] And if you wish, we can overlook the matter." So the man said: "Please overlook it, O Commander of the Believers! I will never mention it again."